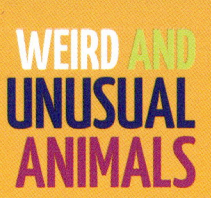

SEA DRAGONS

by Wendy Perkins

AMICUS HIGH INTEREST • AMICUS INK

Amicus High Interest and
Amicus Ink are imprints of Amicus
P.O. Box 1329, Mankato, MN 56002
www.amicuspublishing.us

Copyright © 2018 Amicus. International copyright reserved in all countries. No part of this book may be reproduced in any form without written permission from the publisher.

Library of Congress Cataloging-in-Publication Data
Names: Perkins, Wendy, 1957- author.
Title: Sea dragons / by Wendy Perkins.
Description: Mankato, Minnesota : Amicus High Interest, [2018] | Series: Weird and unusual animals | Audience: K to grade 3. | Includes bibliographical references and index.
Identifiers: LCCN 2016038831| ISBN 9781681511597 (library binding) | ISBN 9781681521909 (pbk.) | ISBN 9781681512495 (ebook)
Subjects: LCSH: Seadragons--Juvenile literature.
Classification: LCC QL638.S9 P47 2018 | DDC 597/.679--dc23
LC record available at https://lccn.loc.gov/2016038831

Photo Credits: tets/Shutterstock background pattern; aaltair/Shutterstock cover, 4-5; Alex Mustard/Nature Picture Library/Alamy Stock Photo 2; Arthit Somsakul/Getty 6-7; AquariusPhotography/Shutterstock 8-9; JaGr19/iStock; Heidi's Pics/Shutterstock 12-13; Alex Mustard/Getty 14-15; Fred Bavendam/Minden Pictures/National Geographic Creative 16-17; Karen Gowlett-Holmes/Getty 19; Warwick Sloss/NPL/Minden Pictures 20-21; powerofforever/iStock 22

Editor: Wendy Dieker
Designer: Aubrey Harper
Photo Researcher: Holly Young

Printed in the United States of America

HC 10 9 8 7 6 5 4 3 2 1
PB 10 9 8 7 6 5 4 3 2 1

TABLE OF CONTENTS

A Tiny Dragon   5
Leafy Flaps   6
Floating Along   9
Keeping Safe   10
Slow Motion   13
Slurp!   14
Number One Dad   17
Hatching Eggs   18
Growing Dragons   21

A Look at Sea Dragons   22
Words to Know   23
Learn More   24
Index   24

A TINY DRAGON

Near Australia, a creature swims in the water along the shore. It looks like a tiny dragon. But it doesn't spit fire. What is it? It is a fish. It is called a sea dragon.

Weird but True
Sea dragons are not lizards. They are fish cousins to sea horses.

LEAFY FLAPS

Sea dragons have flaps on their body. The flaps look like leaves. They match the plants that grow along the rocky shore.

Weird but True
Leafy sea dragons have many flaps. Weedy sea dragons have just a few.

FLOATING ALONG

Sea dragons float and drift like **seaweed**. They look more like a plant than a fish. This helps them hide from **predators**.

KEEPING SAFE

Some animals do find sea dragons. They also find sharp **spines** on the sea dragon. Ouch! Sea dragons have bony plates instead of scales. They protect the sea dragon's body.

Weird but True
A weedy sea dragon is about as long as a 10-year-old's arm. A leafy sea dragon is a little smaller.

SLOW MOTION

Sea dragons are very slow swimmers. They only have a few tiny fins on their head and back. They fan these fins back and forth to steer. Sea dragons seem to just **drift**.

Weird but True
It would take about a half hour for a sea dragon to swim the length of an Olympic pool.

SLURP!

When it's time to eat, sea dragons slurp up food. They suck tiny shrimp into their mouths. Sea dragons don't have teeth. They swallow their food whole. Gulp!

NUMBER ONE DAD

A male sea dragon takes care of the eggs. He has a **brood patch** under his tail. The female presses the eggs onto the patch. He holds up to 300 eggs there. He keeps them safe.

HATCHING EGGS

After one to two months, the eggs hatch. A few babies pop out at a time. It takes about two days for all the eggs to hatch.

Weird but True
Baby sea dragons are called **fry**.

GROWING DRAGONS

Baby sea dragons are the size of your fingernail. They grow for two years. Then they are adults. They swim in the sea for about 10 years. They have a long dragon life.

A LOOK AT SEA DRAGONS

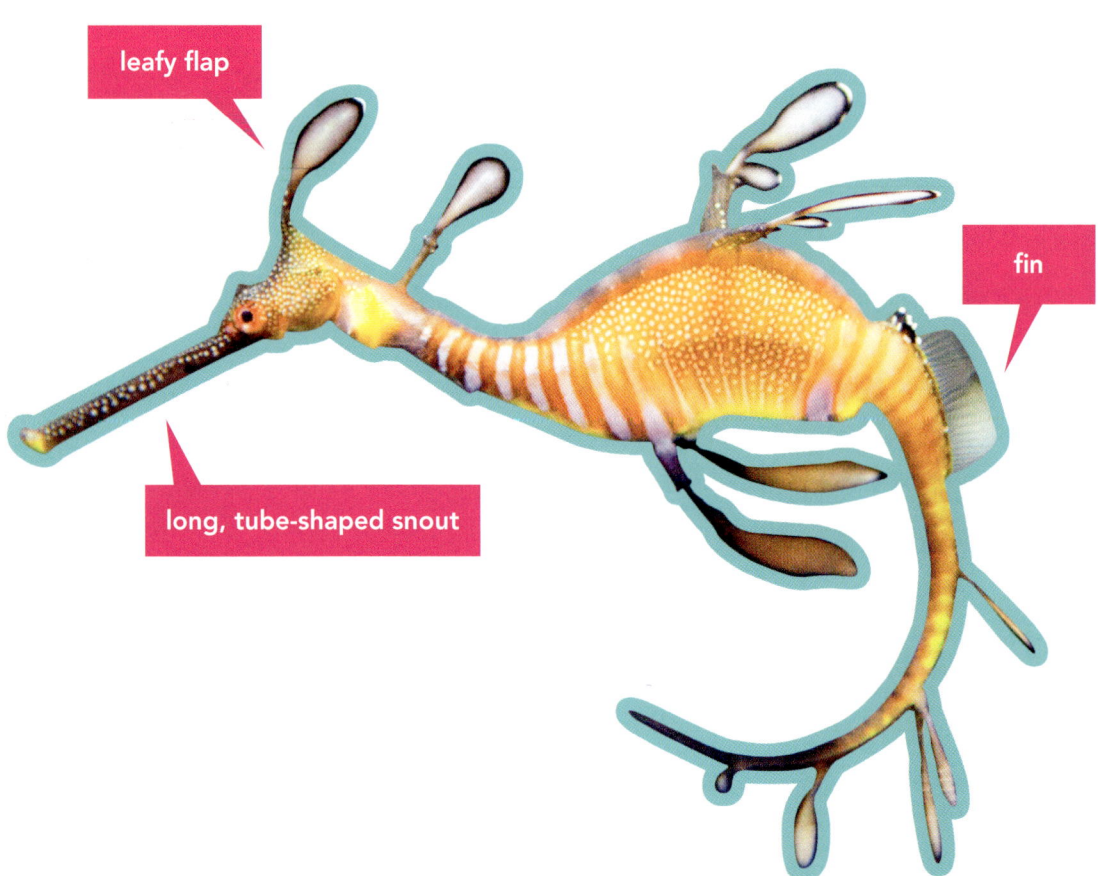

WORDS TO KNOW

brood patch – a place under the male's tail where eggs are kept until they hatch

drift – to float along with no direction

fry – a baby fish

predator – an animal that hunts and eats other animals

seaweed – a kind of plant that grows underwater in the ocean

spine – a hard, sharp, pointy body part

LEARN MORE

Books
McDowell, Pamela. *Sea Dragons*. Ocean Life. New York: AV2 by Weigl, 2012.

Meister, Cari. *Sea Dragons*. Life Under the Sea. Minneapolis: Bullfrog Books, 2015.

Websites
Aquarium of the Pacific: Leafy Seadragons
www.aquariumofpacific.org/onlinelearningcenter/species/leafy_seadragon

National Geographic: Leafy and Weedy Sea Dragon
http://animals.nationalgeographic.com/animals/fish/sea-dragon/

INDEX

bony plates 10

eating 14
eggs 17, 18

fins 13
flaps 6

habitat 5, 6
hiding 9

leafy sea dragon 6, 10

predators 9

size 10, 21
spines 10
swimming 13, 21

weedy sea dragon 6, 10

Every effort has been made to ensure that these websites are appropriate for children. However, because of the nature of the Internet, it is impossible to guarantee that these sites will remain active indefinitely or that their contents will not be altered.